D1267905

PRAYER

Intimate Communication

John Wimber

VMI
Vineyard Ministries International

Copyright © 1997 by John Wimber   All rights reserved

No part of this book may be reproduced or transmitted in any form or by any means, electronic or mechanical, including photo-copying, recording, or by any information storage and retrieval system, without permission in writing from the publisher:

Vineyard Ministries International
P.O. Box 17998
Anaheim, CA. 92817

Printed in the United States of America.

All Scripture quotations, unless otherwise indicated, are from the THE HOLY BIBLE, NEW INTERNATIONAL VERSION. Copyright © 1973, 1978, 1984 by International Bible Society. Used by permission of Zondervan Publishing House. All rights reserved.

ISBN 0-9651509-3-3

Edited by Ruth Henderson.

Cover and book design by Mike Rutland/MDR Design.

FIRST EDITION

Library of Congress Cataloging-in-Publication Data
Wimber, John R.
    Prayer: Intimate Communication
        p.   cm.
    ISBN 0-9651509-3-3
    1. Spiritual Life. 2. Theology, Doctrinal—Prayer.
    I. Wimber, John   II. Title

---

97 98 99 10 9 8 7 6 5 4 3 2 1

This edition is printed on acid-free paper that meets the American National Standards Institute Z.39.48 Standard.

Prayer

Intimate Communication With God

And he walks with me and he talks with me, and he tells me I am his own.

And the joy we share as we tarry there, none other has ever known.

In the Garden

These verses from one of my favorite hymns beautifully express the intimacy we can have with God the Father and the Lord Jesus. I picture myself strolling along with Jesus in a garden, talking about everything that's on my heart and listening to what he wants to tell me.

That, in a nutshell, is what prayer is supposed to be like.

Being intimate with the Father, talking to him throughout the day, sharing my deepest feelings and thoughts with him—that's the kind of interchange God wants to have with me (and you) on a continual basis. Our heavenly Father is glad to hear from us and eager to participate in the give and take of prayer.

Intimate prayer is a great antidote to what sociologists tell us is one of the most common maladies affecting Americans today— acute loneliness.

I know there are many ways to pray and communicate with God. But I want to emphasize intimate prayer as an on-going lifestyle that makes a vital connection to God. Isn't that what we're all after?

Intimacy with God doesn't necessarily require spending several hours in prayer each day. I've read many books about prayer warriors. One or two of those guys almost caused me to quit praying entirely after I read the story of their lives. Some of them prayed eight hours a day. They grew calluses on their knees from praying so long. Can you imagine that? I felt, after reading their books, that if that's what was required in order to be an ardent and enthusiastic warrior for the Lord, I was in trouble.

But reading their biographies did inspire me, so as a young Christian, I decided I was going to get up early in the morning and pray. I started setting the alarm at four a m. During the next two weeks I discovered that I could fall asleep in any position: standing, kneeling, sitting, rolling over, clinging to the alarm… I got so discouraged.

I felt as if I was trying to become a spiritual body builder, and I thought, "Lord, I can't get there from here."

Along the way the Lord began speaking to me concerning prayer. He taught me that intimacy with God isn't measured by the length of time I spend on my knees each day. For me, intimate prayer is a continual conversation with God that lasts throughout the day.

Intimate prayer is vital and important, but to fully enter into it, we must first understand the basis for this type of prayer.

Someone once described prayer as an adventure. It is that. But prayer is also the door to a deep and satisfying relationship with our heavenly Father. Intimate prayer can open that door.

Intimacy With God

> *Do not leave my cry unanswered.*
> *Whisper words of truth in my heart.*
> *For you alone speak truth.*
>
> Saint Augustine

Intimacy begins with personal relationship. You can't be emotionally intimate with someone you don't know.

The New Testament gives us a glimpse into the intimate relationship between the Father and the Son. Even after a full day of preaching, healing, casting out demons, dealing with hostile religious leaders, and hearing of the death of a loved one, Jesus couldn't wait to head off by himself and spend the whole night talking with his Father (Matt. 14:23). He loved to be alone with his Dad.

God has something similar in mind for you and me. The joy of the Son was to do the will of the Father. It is our joy to do the will of the Father and the Son. In doing so, we fulfill the purposes of God in this world, part of which is to develop an intimate relationship with you and me.

Have you ever watched your kids playing out in the backyard? You knew everything they did but they still told you about it. It was fun reliving it with them. Your spiritual Father enjoys the same kinds of interaction. It pleases him to talk to you and to hear from you. He likes to hear your perspective on the things that have happened in your life.

Intimacy with the Father and the Son

A common mentality today that is expressed in much of our theology, says, in effect, if you have the right standing before God, and if you know the right scripture, and you quote it properly back to God in a certain manner, then you'll get the results you want. In effect, you can tell God what to do.

That teaching, in my opinion, violates the nature of intimacy. It changes the nature of the relationship from a child climbing in his Father's lap, to an attorney standing before a judge and arguing for a position you're holding.

Prayer begins and ends in relationship with

God. It has to do with the very relationship Jesus had with the Father. In this relationship we can come as his children and say, "Daddy, I've got a need. I've got a problem." David in the Psalms is a good example. He goes to God when he is happy, when things are going well. But he also goes to God when he is depressed and confused. David, the man after God's heart, had intimacy with God.

Intimacy must begin with an intimate understanding of who you are talking to. As a young Christian I had the misconception of God the Father as someone rather austere and far off in the heavens. I had the notion that one of the reasons that Jesus sat before the throne of God all the time was that he had to appease God because God really wasn't happy with all these rascals that Jesus was bringing home. Jesus, I thought, had to talk the Father into it like some children do with their parents. Well, Scripture doesn't teach anything like that.

I wasn't the first ever to struggle with a wrong understanding of who God is. In the times of Isaiah, Israel was told, "Here is your God!" (Is. 40:9) as if they, too, had forgotten God's essential character. Isaiah then described God with two striking but complementary word pictures.

First, Isaiah describes God as a powerful King who rules and reigns and is in control of every circumstance of life. "See, the Sovereign LORD comes with power, and his arm rules for him (v. 10).

Then Isaiah describes God as a tender and gentle Shepherd, caring for and protecting his flock so that they have all they need. "See, … He tends his flock like a shepherd: He gathers the lambs in his arms and carries them close to his heart; he gently leads those that have young" (v. 11).

Sandwiched between these two graphic pictures of power and protection, control and care, majesty and tenderness, are the words, "his reward is with him, and his recompense accompanies him." In other words, when you come to know God rightly, that relationship is all the reward you need. Knowing the Father is our reward. Intimacy with God flows from rightly knowing him and is its own reward because it leads to an ever deepening intimacy. "But as for me, the nearness of God is my good." the Psalmist emphasizes (Psalm 73:28 NASB).

The Bible teaches that Jesus Christ came at the Father's beckoning and direction to do the work of the Father and extend the Father's love to the world. He did so through his death and resurrection which was in the Father's heart and mind from the very outset. Jesus' death, resurrection, and ascension opened the way

into God's presence to enjoy intimacy with him
(Heb. 10:19-24). So when you come as a child
of God to the Father in prayer, you need to see
yourself as completely welcome in his presence
because that's the way our Father sees it.

Intimacy With God Leads to Doing the Works of Christ

Jesus only spoke the words of the Father.
So whenever he spoke, and wherever it's
written down, we have the recorded words of
the Father. Through intimacy with the Father,
we are able to enter into the life of Christ and
do the works of Christ.

He has called us to do *his* works—it's all a
part of the relationship he wants with us. "For
we are God's workmanship, created in Christ
Jesus to do good works, which God prepared
in advance for us to do" (Eph. 2:8-10). Because
you can come to God anytime, it is possible to
continually ask him to show you the good
works that he has prepared ahead for you to
walk in. In asking for God's guidance in what to
pray for, I've experienced asking for things
beyond my own ability to expect to happen.
But as the Lord Jesus filled me with faith, the
very thing that I thought was too incredible to

happen, has happened.

A good example is the building the Vineyard Christian Fellowship of Anaheim now occupies. The day before we used the sanctuary for the first time back in 1991 the Lord reminded me of the many different buildings I had asked him for in the past, buildings he had *not* given us. I got out my calculator and added up the square footage of all those other buildings. It hit me like a ton of bricks— the new facility could hold all those other buildings put together!

The Ebb and Flow of Intimacy

There's an ebb and flow in all relationships. There are times when I'm much more intimate with the Father, and times when I'm much less intimate with him. There are times when I feel like he loves me, and there are other times when everything in me denies that.

Relationship with God is like a relationship with a person—it must be maintained and nurtured. It's like a good garden—it's got to be worked at if you want to keep it nice. If you ignore your relationship, it will cool off. If you work at it, it'll warm up. And so it is in a relationship with God.

Even though we often fall way short of

representing Christ to the world in a positive way, that still doesn't change our relationship with God. It may change our *enjoyment* of the relationship, but it doesn't change the relationship from the Father's point of view.

Feelings of Unworthiness Block Intimacy

It's hard to feel intimate with God when I feel unworthy. The devil knows this and "encourages" me to think about all of my limitations.

Just as I'm starting to pray, the devil will say, "You're a sinner." Hard to argue with that one. More often than not, though, I make the mistake of listening further. "Remember what you did yesterday? Remember the thoughts you had? The things you said? What right do you have to talk to a holy God?"

He's got a point, I say to myself, I have sinned. And because of my sin, I really don't have any basis for approaching God.

Before I know it, my prayer is snuffed out because I listen to the deception of the enemy.

The way out of that lie and back to intimacy with God is simple—be honest. Intimacy in prayer begins with honesty. Call sin by its name; don't sugar-coat it with psychological labels or cover it with justifications. Don't let the devil steal your prayer life away by telling you half-truths. Name your sin, confess it, ask forgiveness for it and allow "the blood of Jesus to purify [you] from all sin" (paraphrase of I Jn. 1:9).

In my better moments, when Satan throws the "You can't pray—you're a rotten sinner" line in my face, I say, "Don't tell me about it. Dad handles the Complaint Department." I recognize that I don't have any basis for praying in and of myself, but my Father has assured me that I can enter into his presence with confidence because of the blood of his Son. (Heb. 10:19-22). I thank God for his Word. I would've quit praying a long time ago if it weren't for the Bible.

The Value God Places on Us

This may sound strange but I've never really gotten it straight why God chose me in the first place. I'm always half-expecting the Lord to show up and say, "Everybody who's going to heaven, take one step forward." Then he'll look at me and say, "What are you doing here, Wimber?"

But God, not desiring that any should perish (John 3:16) placed value on me when I saw no value in myself. This passage from

Paul's letter to the believers in Ephesus has helped me over the years to see the value God places on me:

> For he chose us in him before the creation of the world to be holy and blameless in his sight. In love he predestined us to be adopted as his sons through Jesus Christ, in accordance with his pleasure and will—to the praise of his glorious grace, which he has freely given us in the One he loves.
>
> In him we have redemption through his blood, the forgiveness of sins, in accordance with the riches of God's grace that he lavished on us with all wisdom and understanding.
>
> And he made known to us the mystery of his will according to his good pleasure, which he purposed in Christ, to be put into effect when the times will have reached their fulfillment—to bring all things in heaven and on earth together under one head, even Christ.
>
> In him we were also chosen, having been predestined according to the plan of him who works out everything in conformity with the

purpose of his will, in order that we, who were the first to hope in Christ, might be for the praise of his glory.

And you also were included in Christ when you heard the word of truth, the gospel of your salvation. Having believed, you were marked in him with a seal, the promised Holy Spirit who is a deposit guaranteeing our inheritance until the redemption of those who are God's possession—to the praise of his glory. (1:1-14)

This passage is a great antidote to "worm" theology, isn't it? God says about you and me—and every believer—that *In Christ* he *chose* us before time began (before we did anything to deserve or forfeit relationship with him), he *adopted* us as beloved children into his family, he *made provision* for our main problem—sin, and he *assured* us that we have an unbelievable inheritance, guaranteed by a down payment beyond measure—the Holy Spirit himself. So the next time Satan calls you a worm, read these verses, and enjoy who you are *In Christ*.

The Basis for Intimate Prayer

I don't have intimate prayer with the Father based on my good attitudes or actions. I come on the basis of his righteousness. He justified, established, sanctified, called, saved and brought me into the same relationship that he had with the Father before the world was founded. He hears me when I call on him.

Jesus gave his disciples a new and sweeping promise in his last, intimate time with them in the Upper Room (cf. Jn 14). Six times during that talk Jesus repeated this promise, "Then the Father will give you whatever you ask" as you pray "in my name." God answers prayers prayed in the name of Jesus. But what does it mean to pray in the name of Jesus? Can I ask for *anything* I want?

The name of Jesus is like a check that can be cashed in by those who have been called by his name. When you go to the bank with a check, it's the signature on that check that makes it cashable. The signature guarantees that you can draw on the resources in the account. If you have the wrong name but the right check, you can't cash it. It's the name that makes it possible to cash it.

When we pray "in Jesus' name," we pray as his representative; we ask for the things that he would ask for if he were in our situation.

Praying in the name of Jesus is praying for the things of Jesus.

So we pray in the name of Jesus. You can't get answers to your prayers any other way. Not in the name of Mohammed, Buddha or the Republican Party. You have to ask in the name of Jesus Christ. That's the only name that God honors.

It amazes me that I can have an intimate relationship with God, knowing who I am and what I've been. I wouldn't even speak to myself if I were him. But he loves me and has demonstrated it so many ways that it's now beyond question in my mind. I know his love. I know his generosity. I know his faithfulness. And knowing him, I trust him. I believe him when he says he wants an intimate relationship with me.

How we perceive God profoundly affects how we come to him in prayer and how intimate we are with him. Shortly before going to the cross, Jesus prayed, "I have made you known to them, and will continue to make you known *in order that the love you have for me may be in them.*" Jesus prayed that God would love you the way he loves his Son. We've been offered that relationship.

The Importance of Intimacy

I am daily continuing in prayer and expecting the answer. Be encouraged with fresh earnestness to give yourself to prayer, only be sure that you ask for things that are for the glory of God.

George Mueller

I was raised as an only child in a household where my mother was divorced and had remarried. Both she and my stepfather worked. When I was around five, I discovered music. It became my refuge, my passion. By the time I was eighteen, I had learned to play about seventeen instruments.

On a typical day, I would head home after school and practice for six or seven hours. This was my routine every day of every week. No wonder I didn't develop many social skills! It was hard to develop social graces with an instrument stuck in my mouth or lap.

And except for the fact of the grace of God and Carol, my wife, I probably wouldn't have ever learned how to be intimate with anybody. Carol has helped me see that being tough is okay, but being emotionally invulnerable isn't. It is scary being vulnerable with her, with God, with friends, but I am so much more human when I am.

In our culture we are trained to be, in a very real sense, distanced from those we are intimate with. Our Western civilization comes from a somewhat stilted, formal history and background. As a result, many of us grow up in households where we share furniture and food with family members, but we never really learn how to be intimate with them.

Often, when I'm in a small group, the Holy Spirit will prompt someone to prophesy over me and say that I'm God's "Beloved."

Everything in my system says "Tilt!" I can't receive that because I know how disobedient and hard hearted I am. For God to call me his "Beloved" just doesn't compute. Yet he keeps telling me that because he's trying to help me understand that he means it.

My intimacy with God has nothing to do with my performance; it has everything to do with his commitment to me. Jesus Christ offers you and me the relationship that he had with the Father before the world was formed (that's part of what Jesus prayed in John 17:21-26, and Jesus gets his prayers answered). By his blood, and as a result of the sacrifice that Jesus made on the cross, you and I have a bold, free, fearless access to the Father, just like Jesus did (Eph. 2:14-18, 3:12). We've been born again of the Spirit of God.

Jesus' Intimacy with the Father

Jesus' intimacy with the Father set the pattern for us to follow. He demonstrated this intimacy in the way he talked to his Father in prayer. Jesus didn't use formal, religious language when he prayed. He used dinner table talk of a close family. "Abba" is an Aramaic word most often translated as "Father." But that is a bit stiff and does not really nuance the meaning. When Jesus prayed "Abba," he was really saying "Daddy"—a special term of endearment.

Jesus looked forward to his prayer times. He would heal crowds of sick people, feed the hungry, debate the Pharisees and then slip away to spend time praying in some secluded place.

After Jesus healed a man covered with leprosy, Luke records that "...the news about [Jesus] spread all the more, so that crowds of people came to hear him and to be healed of their sicknesses. But Jesus often withdrew to lonely places and prayed" (Luke 5:15,16).

When we first come to know Christ, many of us simply don't know how to be intimate with God in prayer. Since we often don't know what to do with this business of prayer, we lapse into repeating familiar little phrases. Have you ever prayed regularly with children over the dinner table, and they say "amen" and dig in, *just* before you finish? We're pretty predictable in our prayer lives.

Think for a moment about your closest relationships. You've reached a level of love and trust with these people which allows you to be truly transparent with them. In order to develop an intimate prayer life with God, we need to be transparent, that is completely honest and open with him. "Father," you might say, "I have something in me that resists you. I have a heart that's prone to wander. I have appetites and desires that are contrary to your appetites and desires. I have a will that resists you. All of these things, Father, would stop me from becoming more like you. In spite of all those things, I want you to help me to become like you."

He loves to answer a prayer like that!

In John 13-17, Jesus speaks openly about his relationship with his Father (especially in chapter 14-17). I believe that Jesus was saying, "This same open, loving, intimate relationship that I have with my Father is the same relationship that we can have together." I can support that assertion from these chapters, but unfortunately do not have the space here. Maybe this can whet your appetite to study this magnificent portion of Scripture for yourself.

Jesus also talks to his disciples in a way that beautifully demonstrates the intimate relationship he had with them. This is a dynamic and profound passage, filled with love, tenderness and pathos. Jesus has spent three years with these men, and he is now just hours from the end of his life on earth with these friends.

In spite of knowing that Peter—one of his closest companions—would deny him, Judas would betray him and Thomas would doubt him, Jesus drew them all close with his words and bared his heart. Notice how Jesus used the emotion laden word pictures of an abandoned orphan and the pain of a woman in child birth (14:18, 16:21) to communicate his heart. I always read this passage slowly—it feels like I'm in a holy place.

In John 14:1 Jesus begins by saying, "Do not let your hearts be troubled. Trust in God;

trust also in Me." That's one of the most profound statements in all of history. Jesus equates belief in God with belief in him, thereby equating himself with God.

It's possible to put on an act in public and fool some. But you and I know we can't fool our friends, at least not for any length of time. Ever been camping? If you have, you know what it was like for Jesus and the apostles for those three years. The twelve knew him the best. They had ministered together, shared all their meals, slept side by side, and suffered the hardships of traveling together. A person's real character comes out in those circumstances.

What had the disciples seen of Jesus' character, what had they observed over the three years? They had heard him preach and teach from Sidon to Jericho, had seen the miracles, the feeding of the multitudes; they had seen him walk on water, speak to the elements and watch them come under his control; he demonstrated again and again that he was the Lord over all creation.

They knew what it was like to work all day together in the heat of the Middle-Eastern sun and then for Jesus to stay up all night praying. Some of them had seen Jesus transformed in a marvelous and supernatural way. They had seen visitations from historic (dead) people. They had heard Jesus defend his Messiahship and dumfound the most brilliant minds of Israel.

Yet here they are at this dinner together, and Jesus says, "Do not let your hearts be troubled. Trust in God; trust also in me. In my Father's house are many rooms; if it were not so, I would have told you. I am going there to prepare a place for you. And if I go and prepare a place for you, I will come back and take you to be with me that you also may be where I am (John 14:1-2).

"Trust in God," Jesus said, just days before he was to die a horribly painful death.

"Trust also in me." Jesus is baring his soul to these men, as to us. This is true intimacy. When I read this passage I take it to heart, because it was meant for me, too.

Intimate Prayer in the Bible

There are prayers of startling intimacy throughout the Bible. Many of the significant prayers in the Bible were the personal, intimate cries of the heart, only audible to the God they were intended for.

We don't know what Isaac prayed to the Lord on behalf of his barren wife Rebekah. Throughout twenty-five years of pastoral ministry, my heart has broken for many couples who have agonized for a baby. The pain of barrenness is palpable. Rebekah knew that pain of barrenness, and Isaac shared it. He knew how much bearing a child meant to her. All we know is that he prayed.

And we know the Lord answered his prayer. Rebekah became pregnant. (See Gen. 25:21.) I'm sure if we could hear that prayer, we would hear a simple and unadorned request—one man asking the one God for one thing on behalf of the one woman he loved.

The Psalms are full of David's heartfelt prayer-songs. Talk about intimate! He sings about his doubts, his fears, his sins, his confusion. David also sings about God's goodness and faithfulness. It's clear the Lord enjoyed their relationship. After all, God called David "a man after my own heart."

Some of David's prayer-songs were, especially when I was a new believer, a bit too intimate for me. How could such a mighty warrior say those things I would ask myself. While reading a particularly intimate psalm, I'd stop right in the middle and say, "Nobody talks like that! Nobody says things like that!" I wasn't aware in the those early days that psalms were songs and while people may not talk like that, they do sing like that. I should know—it happened to me.

One night, dead tired after a particularly

arduous work week, I had just pulled into the driveway when my son Tim came bounding out of the house. "Dad," he said, "One of your friends is waiting for you at the airport." "What?" I growled back. "You're supposed to there already. He's been waiting an hour."

"Lord, no," I prayed. I was thoroughly exhausted. Just the thought of fighting Friday night traffic through Los Angeles sent me over the cliff. I ranted and raved for a few minutes. Poor Tim. I threw my briefcase on the floor and headed out the door for the airport.

Twenty minutes into the drive the fog of frustration lifted. I knew I had to apologize to my son for my outburst. I pulled off the freeway and found a phone booth. I felt a little better after the call, but not much.

The Lord wasn't through with me.

I felt sorry for myself and put out, and I told the Lord all about it. As I poured out my heart to him, I felt the Holy Spirit meeting my travel-worn spirit and soothing, comforting and renewing me. Tears came to my eyes as I refocused on God's goodness and faithfulness to me.

Suddenly—and with almost no effort—the words and the tune to "Isn't He" were there on my lips and I sang it over and over on the rest of the trip to the airport. "Isn't He Beautiful, Beautiful, isn't He? Son of God, Prince of

Peace, Isn't He? Isn't He?"

You could say it made the trip worthwhile!

So, in the beginning, I had great difficulty relating to David and to that level of intimacy. Reading David now challenges me to grow ever more willing to bare my heart wide open to God.

If not for the Word of God I would be unable to deal with those fears about being inadequate and insincere, those irrational fears about separation from God. And if it weren't for the written Word of God I would have nothing to work with in helping me to deal with the substantial fact God loves me in spite of my performance. He loves me in spite of the things that I am, and the things I've been.

As I've learned the Word of God my concept of who God is and how he can change me has grown, and at the same time my intimacy and relationship with him has grown. If it weren't for that love, for that power of God's grace on my heart and life, there'd be no potential for me ever improving.

Abiding In Intimate Prayer

It is as though God has a favorite food. When we pray, he smells the aroma from the kitchen as you prepare his special dish. When God hungers for some special satisfaction He seeks out a prayer to answer. Our prayer is the sweet aroma from the kitchen ascending up into the King's chambers making him hungry for the meal. But the actual enjoyment of the meal is his own glorious work in answering our prayers.

John Piper
The Pleasures of God

In the Gospel of John, Jesus talks about an absolutely essential element for a quality prayer life. "If you remain in me and my words remain in you, ask whatever you wish, and it will be given you" (15:7). The word "remain" here means to live in Jesus, to take your sustenance from him, dwell with him, give yourself over to the process of living there.

If you remain in him, his words will remain in you and be dynamic and powerful.

The result? "...Ask whatever you wish, and it will be given to you." You say, "You mean all I have to do is live in Jesus and his words live in me and then I can ask anything I want to?"

If you're remaining in Jesus and his words are abiding or remaining in you, you'll be asking on a different level and a different plane. Remaining or abiding in intimate prayer means you will care about those things that God cares about and pray the prayers of faith that he already wants to answer.

Abiding in obedience

Abiding or remaining is directly related to obeying. 1 John 3:22-24 says that we can have confidence because we,

> ... receive from him anything we ask, because we obey his commands and do what pleases him. And this is his command: to believe in the name of his Son, Jesus Christ,

and to love one another as he commanded us. Those who obey his commands live in him, and he in them. And this is how we know that he lives in us: We know it by the Spirit he gave us.

So there's a relationship between abiding in Jesus and obeying Jesus. It is all wrapped up in the Person of Jesus and a relationship with him that's intimate and eternal. It is imperfect on my part but perfect on his part; perfectly provisioned on his part, imperfect in response on my part.

Saving us isn't enough—he wants to love us. Taking us to heaven wouldn't be enough—he wants to be our intimate friend. He wants to talk with us, be with us, enjoy us. He has a sense of humor, too. (If he saved me, you know he has a sense of humor.)

A Secret Prayer Life

God wants us to develop a secret prayer life with him. Why do I say that? Look at Jesus. Although he taught on public prayer, Jesus repeatedly stressed in his ministry this business of private prayer. "But when you pray, go into your room, close the door and pray to your

Father, who is unseen. Then your Father, who sees what is done in secret, will reward you" (Matt. 6:6). With prayer comes a reward.

Jesus also commands us to, "Be careful not to do your `acts of righteousness' before men, to be seen by them. If you do, you will have no reward from your Father in heaven" (6:1).

The key to intimacy in this passage is doing the things dictated by your own heart as you relate to God—don't do them for the applause, or approval, or the honor of men. Do them for God alone.

That's a powerful principle. Many of us play out our lives for the blessing and approval of others. If you do it for the Father, with his approval in mind, with his response in mind, you will naturally develop that intimacy with him that can bring such delight.

He values the privacy of prayer. A major part of what is accomplished in the world today occurs "with the door closed," one-on-one with God. Cultivate that intimacy and linger before the Lord in prayer. Allow him to help you formulate your requests and petitions.

Nurture your "secret history" with the Lord. Make time for listening to him as well as for talking to him about all that is in your heart.

As a young Christian I used to pray over and over again, "Oh, God, make me strong. Help me to resist temptation." God finally spoke to me one night (an impression in my mind) and said, "You're not going to become strong... ever." That response caught me completely off guard because I believed that someday I was going to have myself "together."

The Holy Spirit spoke to me and said, "John, just how strong do you want to become seeing you can do nothing without Me?"

The Lord gave me the verse, "I am the vine; you are the branches. If a man remains in me and I in him, he will bear much fruit; apart from me you can do nothing" (Jn. 15:5). The Lord used that verse to tell me, "You'll never be strong. I am to be strong. I'm all the strength you'll ever need." That dependence is part of the relationship of intimacy that he desires with us.

Praying in the Spirit

A few years ago, I had the opportunity to visit Jackie Pullinger-To, a woman doing a phenomenal work among drug addicts in Hong Kong. I wanted to know how she was able to lead so many people to the Lord, and meet so many needs of the new believers as they struggled to lead a new life in Christ. Friends of mine accompanied her as she went about her day on the streets and buses of Hong Kong.

They discovered that Jackie spends her day walking the narrow lanes and alleys of Hong Kong, praying in the Spirit and asking the Father what he is doing, where he is moving, and who needs him most. What a precious example of intimate prayer communication! By simply abiding in Jesus and doing the things the Father shows her to do she has been able to reach hundreds for Jesus.

Studying through I Corinthians 14, you'll discover that praying in the Spirit is a way of communicating and edifying yourself in an intimate connection with God. Scripture says, "And pray in the Spirit on all occasions with all kinds of prayers and requests." (Eph. 6:18a). Paul here is saying that we should pray in a spiritual language as well as pray under the anointing and the initiation of the Holy Spirit.

We are all three dimensional in reflection of the makeup of God. We consist of body, soul and spirit. The body we are well acquainted with; the soul is our mind, intellect and personality which we are also acquainted with; and then we have a spiritual dimension. As a result of being born again, the Spirit of God comes into us, indwells and reinvigorates us. He renews our spirit, brings it to life as the Scripture says. So the result is body, soul and born-again spirit.

Now we know that our mind operates our

tongue, or at least it should. On occasion we don't get our mind in gear before our tongue starts talking. But did you realize that your spirit can run your tongue the same way your mind can?

There is a tremendous dimension of self-edification in praying in the Spirit. When I am at a low point one of the ways I've found to get replenished is to go off by myself, read the Word and pray in the Spirit. As I pour out my heart to God in my most intimate prayers, I have found I move back and forth between my natural language and spiritual language.

Now I have found there is a fascinating relationship between praying in the Spirit and the revelation of God. There are times when God reveals to me things he wants to change or bring to pass in my own development as well as my loved ones. As I pray in the Spirit, I fix my mind on needs of people and their situations and I pray all that is in my mind and heart. Then when I have exhausted all I know to pray about, I'll begin praying in the Spirit again fixing the person and his or her need in my mind. As I move back and forth from my spiritual language to my natural language many times I find revelation comes.

I have to admit that at first when these revelations began to happen I chalked it up to allowing my imagination to run away with me.

But when those revelations about someone have come about and I have prayed about them and have seen answers, I realized it is a way to reach into the spiritual realm and pull things into the natural realm.

Sometimes when I'm driving along I'll be talking in English to the Lord, and then I go back and forth into a spiritual language because I've learned there is a flow of interpretation that way. I learn things from the Spirit even though my mind is not doing the praying, my spirit is, and insights float up to a cognitive state. To me it is a delightful intimate exchange with God.

Intimate Praise

True heartfelt praise is an integral part of abiding in an intimate relationship with God. I can remember when I was a little boy sitting on my granddaddy's lap and feeling my granddaddy's muscles. I'd say, "You must be the strongest grandpa in the world." And he'd say, "I am." And I believed him because for me, he was. But the difference between my grandpa and my spiritual Father is that he's everything that I ever hoped he would be. My grandpa didn't disappoint me and neither has my spiritual Father.

Praise is simply recounting back to God who he is and what he's done. The benefit is in the recounting. As I praise God, I'm reminded of how awesome he is. I'm also reminded of the many blessings that he has poured out to me because of his generosity and his character.

When I spend time praising God, I've found that my heart is edified or built up. I'm reminded that this eternal God, this mighty God, this wonderful God that I'm talking to, loves *me*. Before the world was ever made that relationship was one that he had always planned for *me* to partake of and to be a part of. "For he chose us in him before the creation of the world" (Eph. 1:4); we were in his plans, his mind, his heart. I still can't get over that!

It's an exciting thing to talk to the God of the universe about how wonderful he is. But there are times when you just want to climb up on his lap and sit and talk to the Father and feel his muscles.

When you come to God with a petition, praise him at the same time. Often in my prayer life I intermix the two. I praise God and then I petition him. Praise lifts my faith level. I remind myself of the nature and track record of God, and his trustworthiness.

Answers to Intimate Prayer

> *If you see God's hand in everything, it is easier to leave everything in God's hands.*
>
> Anonymous

Bert Waggoner, a Vineyard pastor from Houston, Texas, told me about a time when the Lord prompted him to pray intimately for his sons. It was during a time when God was leading Bert and his wife Evelyn to pray for major spiritual breakthroughs for their children.

The family was driving along in the car and their two teenage sons were bickering and putting each other down in the back seat. He told me, "I realized I had let some things get to a point that I knew it was not pleasing to the Lord, and I needed help from the Holy Spirit." Bert began to silently call out to God for help. Within minutes the boys seemed to go from cursing each other to blessing each other.

Right then the Lord spoke to Bert and told

him the enemy had strategies against his boys and to be more vigilant in prayer for them. At the dinner table Bert told his family about God's warning to him that the enemy was going to try to thwart the spiritual break-throughs that they had been praying for and experiencing.

One evening as their thirteen year-old son Reagan was playing on his skateboard, he fell and hurt himself badly. He was bleeding and in a great deal of pain. Both parents began to pray. The bleeding and pain stopped almost immediately. They were so aware of God's presence and at that moment Bert said he felt the Lord warning him that the enemy was going to strike at their other son, Art, and to pray for him immediately. Bert told his wife Evelyn and they prayed for protection over Art and asked God to destroy the strategies of the enemy.

About half an hour later Art called to tell them that he had been in an accident. He had been riding his bike across a field where someone had removed a manhole cover. He was going about very fast when his bike went into the hole and he was thrown off. He sailed through the air and it felt just like he was being borne along by unseen arms. He said, "Dad, it was a miracle—I wasn't hurt at all!" His bike was bent hopelessly into a v-shape, but Art was completely uninjured!

This was very significant to their family. It increased their awareness of their need to be sensitive to pray as the Spirit gives direction. To their family it became like a memorial not only to God's faithfulness, but to his intervening and leading in intercessory prayer.

Unanswered Prayer

No matter how intimate your prayer life is there are times when it seems that God is not answering. Like author C.S. Lewis described upon the death of his wife, "the heavens are leaden." Sometimes I feel like the Lord is not near when trials come my way. I feel like he's far off, that he's broke, and that his resources are rather limited. But that doesn't stop me from still crying out, "Help, Lord!"

Some things that come your way are not God's will or plan for your life. Your enemy planned them, and he's committed to destroying you. But also some things are allowed to come to pass that are for our benefit. We can thank God for those things in the sense that he is a sovereign God and he intends to build up our character and our inner being.

In the last few years my wife and I have

faced some of the hardest things of our lives. I have lived through inoperable cancer, a stroke, and heartbreaking illness in my family. But God in his love and through those circumstances has been teaching me new things.

Troubles will come and go, but a relationship with God is eternal. Rejoicing in the Lord is simply recognizing what he's done for you—what he has provided in Jesus Christ—and for who he is. In reality I can always rejoice, whether I'm in good or bad times because I know they are temporary.

So rejoicing *always* is rejoicing *anyway*. He didn't say, "Be happy always". Dire circumstances develop in our lives and it would be preposterous to even try to pretend we're happy over some things that come our way. In this life, you're going to have some tough times, and things are going to get you down from time to time. You can't just whistle those circumstances away. But like Paul and Silas in prison, (Acts 16:25) you can worship in spite of what the day has brought forth.

Yes, No and Wait!

God has promised he will never leave me nor forsake me. He'll not allow circumstances to get out of control. He is in control of circumstances and these things that come my way are simply the dividends of daily living and are not going to "sink my ship."

Sometimes, I get it so fixed in my mind how I want it to work out, that I don't think it's an answer to prayer until it's worked out that way. Occasionally I've realized that God already answered me but because he didn't do it the way I asked him to do it, I didn't think he answered at all. One of the things I've had to learn in walking out an intimate prayer life is to recognize God's answers, whether "Yes," "No" or "Wait!"

There are times in my life I've had to go to God and I've said, "Lord, just be merciful to me. Do something I don't deserve. Do something beyond anything I could possibly dream of, or even ask for. Do something, Lord, I need your help." God answers those prayers.

I already mentioned how the Lord gave the Anaheim Vineyard Christian Fellowship a building so large that all the other buildings I had been praying for could fit into it. This was a powerful moment in my life. God was showing me that," No, not now," is an answer too. Of course, it would have made me feel better if he had told me that what he had in mind was much bigger and better than what I was asking for. However, my job is and always will be to trust him with any answer he cares to give!

One of the big helps to me was studying the word "hearing" in the Old Testament. When God says in the Old Testament, "He hears," it means he acts, he's already moving on it, he's taken your case in hand.

The Apostle John, after establishing a long history of having his prayers answered, wrote, "This is the confidence we have in approaching God: that if we ask anything according to his will, he hears us. And if we know that he hears us, whatever we ask, we know that we have what we asked of him" (1 John 5:14-15).

So we have confidence that when we pray what is on God's heart, he hears the prayers of the saints, and he's already moving on it, it's well under way. Remembering that when I pray fills my heart with gratitude. I say, "Oh God, you not only hear, you act. And sometimes before I say it, before I even request it, you're already moving on my behalf."

Sin Hinders Answers

There are times when a child of God turns his ear away from the voice of God. He tries to block out the corrections, the companionship, and the commandments of God. Selfishness (James 4:3), an unforgiving spirit (Mat. 6:9-15, Mark 11:24-26), and cherishing or holding on to known sin (Psalm 66:18, Is. 59:2) are examples of sin that hinders answered prayer. A person can harden their heart and refuse to respond to God where he has spoken about specific sin.

Then he wonders, "Why can't I get my prayers answered?" If a child of God is praying for various requests and needs, but there is sin in his life that he or she is embracing, God is not likely to respond to that person's prayer. He often withholds his aid to his children at the point where they are sinning and holding the sin to their breast because that sin hinders relationship and God loves us too much to let us go on in our rebellion.

God, because of his love for us, will withhold our requests because it's a way of dealing with us until we repent and come back to him and get our lives straightened out with him. See, God created us for relationship with him, and he is committed to removing all that hinders that intimacy.

Perhaps you've gone through the motions of repenting; you've prayed and you've said, "Oh God, forgive me!" But there wasn't any peace. And so you begin pursuing after the sin again. And you can't get free from it.

In the meantime you're saying, "God help me not to sin. God help me not to do anymore of this. God help me." But there is no response from God; a silent heaven. And you say, "Well, what's a person to do?"

Quit sinning. Just turn around, cold turkey, and quit doing it and begin obeying God. God's help is already available to say "no" to sin and "yes" to him, but God is waiting for you to add faith to his promises and provision, and respond to his help.

There is a powerful story in the Old Testament of God's promise to enter into the promised land. Israel refused to believe God's promise and wandered for forty years in the wilderness before finally entering. The author of Hebrews uses this example to teach that we believers need to combine faith with the promises of God in order to see them come to pass. Faith, of course, is also a gift from God, but is also something that we actively do; faith is active.

Hebrews states"...but the message they heard was of *no value* to them, because those who heard *did not combine it with faith*" (Heb. 4:2, italics mine). Because God has already provided everything we need, "make every effort to add to your faith" godly responses, including saying "no" to sin (2 Peter 1:2-7).

God will respond to you, and he'll answer your prayers. God has a broader and bigger will than most of us realize. Satan is constantly trying to cut down the perimeter of your desire and belief for the things God would do for you. God's will is to bless you and give you the peace he promised. Respond to God and give him a chance to show you.

God's Way or My Way

God has reminded me repeatedly that I really do want to be obedient to him. I've found myself, from time to time, praying this kind of a prayer, "God, forget about what I've done and said in the last few months. I long to obey You. Help me to resist myself. Help me, Father, learn to obey You."

He seems to be answering that prayer because as I look at the characteristic of my life the last thirty-plus years, I find myself progressively learning to obey him. And it's not so tough. Jesus said it would work out that way. He invited those who feel weary and burdened to come to him and take on his yoke, and then promised to give them rest and refreshment. Jesus then gave the reason why we can obey when he added, "For my yoke is easy and my burden is light." That's Jesus' perspective on life with him... and it's truth.

For most of my life, I've been programmed to believe that if I really got my own way I'd be happy. But the Bible and my experience have taught me that God getting his way makes me happy. And the truth is that I'm learning his way is the only way to go. Even though I really do want to obey, it is a continual struggle.

Jesus says he can do it. He can take you on and do what you cannot do. He said he would initiate it and that he would finish it; that he's the Author and the Finisher of your salvation. And he said he can save you in spite of your-self. I believe it for me and I believe it for you.

Be Anxious For Nothing

Your Father knows what you need before you ask him. Have you ever had the thought, "Well, if the Father knows what I need before I ask him, why ask him?" Because it's in the asking that you get to know him. It's climbing up on his lap and saying, "Daddy, I've got something I want to talk to You about." That brings you and God the Father close together in that intimate communication.

I like to think of one aspect of prayer as a release valve. It's something that I do as a result of anxiety. Now I don't know about you, but there have been times when I knelt down to pray and got up worse off than when I started. That's because when I got through telling God about everything, I realized how bad it really was, and did not leave it with Him. By the time I got through laying out the whole story, I would say, "Oh no! There's no way for You to fix this." But there's nothing further from the truth.

The Lord cares about your most anxious prayers, just like a father cares about his child's anxieties. There are times when my prayers bubble up in desperation like a boiling kettle. I can pull the thing off the fire, cool it down, but if I put it back on the fire again, what's going to happen? The heat's going to cause it to boil again.

Sometimes the fire of your life will cause you to boil. No matter how many times you take it to God, no matter now many times you take it off the fire, you're still in it and it's going to boil again.

That's why Paul picks up this theme in Philippians 4:6 where he says, "Do not be anxious about anything..." What he says there is really better translated, "When overwhelmed with anxiety and circumstances are so dire and so difficult in your life that they're causing this overwhelming anxiety to rise, pray to God."

That means when the pot's boiling over, come and talk again.

Be Thankful In Everything— and Peace Will Come

This is a process, though, so don't quit. Even when I keep taking it back again and putting it on the fire, God is patient. That's why Paul goes on to describe the process, "...but in everything, by prayer and petition, with thanksgiving, present your requests to God."

In every situation (large problem or small, even if you have taken it back hundreds of times) present your requests to God. Notice that small phrase in between, "With thanksgiving." Why is thanksgiving with prayer so important?

When I thank God, even for difficult situations, my focus is turned to God who must intervene and help in order to resolve it, rather than on my limited resources. Oh, I'm not necessarily thankful *about* the hardship, but *in* the hardship. I know that God will somehow use this for my good, that God will develop needed character in my life, or that God will develop in me a more compassionate ministry, among other reasons.

Keep on coming to God; don't give up. "Tell God every detail of your needs in earnest and thankful prayer" (J.B. Phillips). What's the result?

When you come to God in intimate prayer and lay your burdens at his feet, the Bible says there will be a result. "And the peace of God, which transcends all understanding, will guard your hearts and your minds in Christ Jesus."

I can be at peace in times when there is no peace, in circumstances in which I should not have peace. I can be at peace while I'm waiting for him to fulfill his promise to me, which is to meet the need that I've brought to him.

A good example of this comes from the life of Lawrence "Gunner" Payne, the man who led me to the Lord. On the evening of the most agonizing day of his life, when he had just learned of his daughter's murder, his family gathered around the supper table, though no one could really eat much. Father, mother, son, and their remaining daughter linked hands to give thanks for the food. With their grief still fresh Gunner prayed, "Father, we don't understand, but we trust you."

I'm not sure he realized it at the time, but that prayer would dramatically change his life. He was in essence praying the ultimate prayer of faith. He acknowledged his trust in God, and thereby acquiesced to his will.

But will we always experience that peace immediately? There are some circumstances in my life where I have not been able to get any peace. I've gone back again and again. I've gotten tired of praying "Oh, God!" I've gotten humiliated and depressed from talking about it. I've wanted to run away from things, but just couldn't get away from it.

I've discovered you can still have a kind of peace in those circumstances. And it's the peace of being able to come to God and talk about everything. It's the peace of being driven to your knees when circumstances are in control of your life that are dire and difficult.

It's coming to God and saying, "Oh, God, here I am again. Have mercy. Deal with this situation, Father." There is that feeling when the bubbles quiet down; the steam stops; and the heat comes off and that release comes.

Then you can pray, "When I'm going through these valleys, Father, it's so good to know you're on the other side. It's so good when I feel caught in the darkness to know there's light. It's so good when I'm lonely that there's someone, like you, Father, who loves me."

The peace that Gunner demonstrated by that simple prayer was an indication of his intimacy with the Lord. God's promise to him and to us, too, no matter how often we have to come to him, is a peace that the world cannot understand.

Conclusion

I've not yet come to a place where I can pray for two or three hours at a time. Fifteen or twenty minutes is maximum for me at a time. Two to three minutes is normal at a time. But I can pray two to three minutes many times throughout the day. I find as I sleep at night, that I pray. I wake up praying sometimes. I fall asleep praying. I wake up and pray. I go back to sleep and then wake up again and pray some more. I have continual communication with God that way.

I pray often as I talk to people I meet throughout the course of my day. Talking to God has become as natural as breathing to me. It's as much a part of my thought life as any other aspect of my life.

No one becomes an expert at prayer overnight. We all experience false starts and seasons of dryness. You have to just pick yourself up and start all over again. Along the way, God blesses and encourages you and builds a continuity of success in your life. That's what I have found after thirty-three years of attempting to pray. If I had to pray hours and hours on end to go to heaven, I couldn't go. I thank God it's not a requirement.

God has a desire for us to draw close to him. When you petition him, it's his pleasure, his joy to answer your prayers. He enjoys the dialogue you have with him. He looks forward to the times when you and he talk and share. Just like the companionable stroll in the garden in the old hymn, Jesus wants that warm intimacy of close communication with you. He himself is the reward for that kind of prayer.

List of Resources

Bounds, E. M. *The Essentials of Prayer*.
New York, NY: Revell, 1925.

Gordon, S.D. *Quiet Talks on Prayer*.
Uhrichsville, OH: Barbour, 1984.

Lavender, John. *Why Prayers are Unanswered*.
Wheaton, IL: Tyndale, 1980.

Murray, Andrew *The Believer's School of Prayer*.
Minneapolis, MN: Bethany, 1982.

Schuller, Robert H. *Prayer: My Soul's Adventure
With God*.
Nashville, TN: Nelson, 1995.

Christian, Unknown. *The Kneeling Christian*.
Grand Rapids, MI: Zondervan, 1986.

Living With Uncertainty: My Bout With Inoperable Cancer

When John Wimber was diagnosed with a rare and inoperable form of cancer in the Spring of 1993, he faced an unknown future. Living With Uncertainty is his forthright account of how he dealt with that crisis.

This booklet pulls from the lessons John learned through illness and helps us debunk the myth that Jesus gives us a trouble-free life. It is an honest and gripping account of walking through the valley of the shadow of death all the while holding firmly onto the hand of the Lord.

Paperback #B128   **$4.99**

Witnesses for a Powerful Christ: Strengthening the Foundations of Renewal for the 21st Century Church

God has been stirring the church this century in an unprecedented manner. The last 90 years have been characterized by wave after wave of renewal. As with any flood, however, there is the danger of being overwhelmed by the strength of the current.

The flow of renewal, Wimber says, needs to be channeled in order to be effective. To channel the flow of renewal, we must strengthen the foundation of our Christian lives. Christ-centered worship, the Word of God, our Christian walk and our works of righteousness are four banks that channel this flood we call renewal. These banks not only direct the flow of renewal, they also intensify its force.

Paperback #B130   **$4.99**

Beyond Intolerance: Calling the Church to Love & Acceptance

Sarcasm, animosity, character assassination— it all amounts to the same thing—verbal violence. More and more of it is crowding our airwaves, especially on talk radio shows.

Is the church immune from this type of negative discourse? On the contrary, it seems the Body of Christ has absorbed the spirit of intolerance and anger.

John Wimber in his latest booklet reminds us that "Our brother is never our enemy, even when he acts like one." Timely and relevant, this booklet will guide you back to a focus on Christ, his cause and his Church as an antidote to vitriolic exchanges.

Paperback #B133   **$4.99**

Kingdom Evangelism: Proclaiming the Gospel with Power

We all want to be more effective at sharing the Gospel with others. Most of us have tried and failed at using some of the popular approaches.

In this revised and expanded version of his earlier best-selling booklet of the same title, John Wimber, the man who made "signs and wonders" popular, explains how evangelism in the kingdom of God is simply living one's life under the power of the Spirit.

Paperback #B136   **$3.99**

All booklets published by Vineyard Ministries International and currently available. Call **1-800-780-VINE** to place an order or request a catalog of other VMI products or write:

Vineyard Ministries International
P.O. Box 68025
Anaheim, CA 92817